Wayfaring Stranger is like the ancestors coming back sharing wisdom, sharing love, sharing strength in troubled times. What a magnificent achievement she has crafted. We will always need to hear her words.

—Nikki Giovanni,
Poet and Educator

Beautiful, sensitive and powerful!

—Ken Debono,
Artist

The strength and depth is immense! Life experiences only can dictate such feelings.

—John & Lee Fudge,
The Fudge Connection

Wayfaring Stranger

poems

M. Rose Barkley

ISBN: 0-9666760-7-6

Book design and printing by
FALCON BOOKS

Sound Publishing Company
Richmond, Virginia

PRINTED IN THE UNITED STATES OF AMERICA

Dedication

To everyone who has ever reflected on this world and their places in it— Deciding then to contribute whatever it is they sincerely have to offer towards its betterment.

Preface

Alongside my love of the written word is my love of aged things that survive generations (for the most part) unscathed, albeit somewhat out of date. In other words, I enjoy rooting for antiques and memorabilia for the sheer pleasure of adding such momentos to my life-giving it a much needed sense of grounding. And so it was on one such impromptu mission that I came across the picture on the cover of this book. The man and his pose struck me as one might be "struck" by the proverbial Cupid's arrow—instantly I knew he would grace the cover of my very first book of poems...

Study him for even a moment and you immediately regard him as the quintessential "Wayfaring Stranger." The dictionary refers to the word wayfarer as a "traveler, usually by foot." Obviously, the gentleman in this near hundred year old photo is indeed such a traveler (note the well worn appearance of his prominently placed shoe). Yet, beyond his slightly weathered appearance, belies an intensity that reflects in the abruptness of his jaw and the reticence of his pose. He is the embodiment of the "stranger."

The stranger I refer to is the stranger that we all possess within us. That part of us that is the greatest portion of the self, left unnurtured and even ignored out of fear of familiarizing ourselves with our selves—as though knowledge of the self will actually cause harm, instead of prevent it. Or at the very least, minimize it.

It is not a practice many of us undertake, rarely becoming comfortable with the idea. Yet, ironically, it is just that which would deliver us unto ourselves and our sanity if we would so (constantly) endeavor—as it seems this determined man on the cover, who compels our latent voyeuristic tendencies forward—is keenly aware of.

While we stare at his expression, nearly a century old, it appears we are in fact the strangers, peering quizzically into the face of one wayfarer whose glinted eye suggests a transcendent wisdom many search a lifetime for. Therein lies the link of this man to my works, for it is in his very demeanor that I find the essence of what it requires to be one with the self—and even more importantly, to be "ok" with that self.

It is my hope that the reader of these words and those to follow will glean more personal meaning from them than even I could imagine—much like the gentleman gracing the cover of this book has done so timelessly and eloquently for me.

M. Rose Barkley

CONTENTS

Acknowledgments   ix

Reflection

Late July on a Southern City Porch · · · · · · · · 3
Labyrinth · · · · · · · · · · · · · · · · · · · 4
Moments · · · · · · · · · · · · · · · · · · · 5
Chaos · 6
Today's History · · · · · · · · · · · · · · · · 8
Deep Water · · · · · · · · · · · · · · · · · · 9
In View Of A Cup Half-Full · · · · · · · · · · 10
Vestige · · · · · · · · · · · · · · · · · · · 13
Bad News · · · · · · · · · · · · · · · · · · 14
Literary Cog · · · · · · · · · · · · · · · · · 16
Stained Glass Window · · · · · · · · · · · · · 18
Restorations · · · · · · · · · · · · · · · · · 20

Pulse

Rise n' Shine · · · · · · · · · · · · · · · · · 25
Still · 26
Mind Trippin' Stream of Consciousness
In The City On A Friday Evening
Rejuvenating On The Couch · · · · · · · · · · 28
Laughter · · · · · · · · · · · · · · · · · · · 30
New Race-Ism · · · · · · · · · · · · · · · · 31
Deep Cuts · · · · · · · · · · · · · · · · · · 32
Concerto · · · · · · · · · · · · · · · · · · · 37
Love Ballad · · · · · · · · · · · · · · · · · 38
Tight · 40

Compass

The Point · 45
Arbitrary Disparity · · · · · · · · · · · · · · 47
Reason · 50
Wreckages · 52
Molecular Being · · · · · · · · · · · · · · · · 56
A View of Africa · · · · · · · · · · · · · · · · 58
Savior · 59
Reveille · 60
Ms. Liberty's Stance · · · · · · · · · · · · · 62
Flight of The Spirit · · · · · · · · · · · · · · 64
No Woman-Child Cry · · · · · · · · · · · · · 65
Middle Passage · · · · · · · · · · · · · · · · 66
Spiral Pillar · · · · · · · · · · · · · · · · · · 66
Waste Not · · · · · · · · · · · · · · · · · · · 67

Haiku

Skin · 79
Life · 79
Shame · 79
Hope · 80
Homeless · 80
Hands · 80
Addiction · 81
Nigger · 81
Change · 81

Acknowledgements

Thanks to:

The Almighty Creator and Enabler, (The late but forever great) Brian Barkley—Louise, Ralph & Ralph (#3) Barkley, Richard Reid, Toni Morrison, Charles Bibbs, Amiri Baraka, Frances Cress Welsing, Maya Angelou, Oprah Winfrey, Malcolm X, Betty Shabazz, Langston Hughes, Cornel West, Gwendolyn Brooks, Nelson Mandela, Zora Neale Hurston, Frederick Douglass, Marita Golden, Leontyne Price, Marian Anderson, Venus Williams, Tiger Woods, Noel Pointer, Norman Brown, Pat Metheny (& Co.), Chaka Khan, Anita Baker, Elton John, Boney James, Me'Shell Ndegeocello, Seal, Tony Medina, Audre Lorde, bell hooks, Toi Dericotte, Sandi Warren, Robert "Robby" Johnson, Vince "The Madman" Maddox, Vince "The Globe" Spann, Howard Hawkins, Lee "The Fudge Connection" & John Fudge, Frank "The spiritually eccentric" Delphin, Maggie "Ms. Thang" Whang, Eunice Gill, April James, Maysa Leak, Lawrence & Rosalind Money, James & Veria Jefferson, Rosa Belle & Willie "Deak" Walker, Sharon Campbell, Chuck Goetz, The Oliphant Family, Imani Howard, Ken Debono, Gwendolyn Nixon, Kelvin Hanson, Freda Bein, Spike Lee, Iyanla Vanzant, Lauryn Hill, Jewel Kilcher, Patrick

Mamou & The Jazz Poets Society, Tupac Shakur, Lester "Mr. Africa" White, Sheila Rincon, Debra Smith, Ramona Haggerty, Khalil Gibran, Sidney Portier, Ruby Dee, Ozzie Davis, Dorothy Dandridge, Walter Bell and the Latin Jazz Unit, Jada Pinkett-Smith, Josephine Baker, Jimi Hendrix, Robert Frost, Alice Walker, Maxine Waters, Morris Dees, LeAlan Jones, Lloyd Newman, Hannes Cooper, Ralph Wiley, James Baldwin, Stevie Wonder, Patti LaBelle, Freda "Phillygirl" Austin, Earl Beck, Robert "The Boss" Ross, Craig Brumback, and every other person, place or thing that has had a significant impact upon my life.

Special Thanks

To Nikki Giovanni for going the distance with me, believing and encouraging all the while. And for being the awesome spirit you are.

To Susan L. Taylor for personally choosing my work, "Moments" for publication in ESSENCE Magazine. And for generously wielding your joyful powers among us.

I

Reflection

The freest people are also the strongest, for in their quest for truest expressions of self, they risk rejection the most.

Late July On A Southern City Porch

Listening
outside the walls
beyond the doors and
windows

Hearing
shrills
Words spoken-screamed
back and forth
cross-leveled
from person to person
perched atop
a small porch
seeking to capture
breezes
beating their way down
West Marshall Street
as is customary
now that dusk approaches
playing beat the clock
on the last of warmed gusts
before cool takes hold
gliding in the gleeful
shrieks
bringing on the bearable night
and deep breaths
before not so silent
sleep

Labyrinth

Feeling
like a half
completed
project in need of
complete abandonment
idly remaining
barely at peace
feeling
no answers appear
to the voids sought
to fill
their collective complexities
scattered
feeling
deeper than the abysmal air
pockets indiscriminately
found repeatedly
just in time for life
sustainment
once again
gulping hungrily @ unforeseen intervals
reprieving while delaying
the inevitable
until renewed
meaning is found
and life is
living

Moments

I sit thinking
Blinking memories
of You
Blinking
Past images
of You
Thinking
of You
Fondly
Often
Blinking
Back
Tears
Thinking
Of
You

Chaos

Nothing
making sense
noise pervades
silence
disruption is the order
of misunder
standing
Nothing
breeds swiftly
but lack of communication
though screaming
Nothing
is heard through
matching choruses
devoid of wit
embellished with tenacity
as gesturings
paint the air
already thick with one-
sided insistences stifling
as would a sock
in the mouth
of one with a headcold gasping
for breath
repeatedly

in vain
attempting to break
surface waters from leagues deep
left untraveled
on either side
and neither caring
to share the oxygen
choosing instead to die of suffocation
and migraines
One
tragically releasing
the other leaving
Nothing

Today's History

I don't want
back
what I once had
The way it was
no
I don't think so
because I am
here
now
as a result
and there
is a reason
for it all
understood
or not
presently
it will be
revealed
unto me
one page
at a time
until my chapter
closes
or my book is
complete

Deep Water

Oceans
come back in
tidal wave
courses
breaking fast
against old memory
cresting firmly
upon real
i-zations
Shimmering disquieted
atop a still moon's
still shadow leaning
triumphantly over top
an entire body's quivering
length
guiding the way
in darkness

In View of a Cup Half-Full

Excessive thoughts crowd
visions
yet realized
beyond circumstance
I question
mystified
by my own direction
unadorned
with sanctimony
unheard
in my suffering
humanness
unearthed
by inconsistencies
of consciousness
I struggle
balancing con-
tempt & disgust
uneasily
exhibiting outer frustration
not in keeping with
my alienation
brought on
daily
by external realities
some lodged permanently
others
agile enough
to plague

in many places
the scores of forgotten
faces
blank
with paralysis
unaware
even of their own
place
in this
race
for justice
often is unheard
or seen by
the most audible ears
and focused eyes

Finding themselves capable
still
feeling
likewise
unearthed
at the roots
longing for
fertile soil
familiar in its proximity
comforting in its embrace
reliable
in its steadfastness
come
rain or shine
or darkness

making more treacherous
the path
when one's life depends
upon clarity
of consciousness
in order to lead
or follow
so inasmuch as
the sun rises east and sets
west
or seasons do change
things
surrounding us all
their remains
an atmosphere
vast and unrelenting
if left to chance
yet miraculously tilled
ready to harvest
all that we sow
in grand abundance
with only our words and actions
necessary to bear fruit
bitter or sweet
like the longed-for verse
found crouched down low
patiently waiting
in the gut
of a poet

Vestige

Like scabs
that crust over
and heal
wounds
otherwise left
open
to elemental devastation
so goes
the spirit
of one
determined
individual
to endure
regardless
The magnitude
of the odds

Bad News

She told me
outside on
an uncomfortable humid night
as I watched pedestrians
and cars
from my back porch
wishing desperately for rain

And then it came
A deluge
With the news
Betty was dead...
Betty Shabazz
Wife of Malcolm
Phenomenon in her own right

Dead
Gone
No longer standing

And no more would we
bear witness to
the strength
the wisdom
the glory
she alone possessed
yet spread so
generously among us

My bottom lip fell close
to the level of my sinking heart
Missing a breath-
so essential
in the face-glove of humidity
outside
which I now found
less stifling than the circumstances

My tears
blocked
only by the lump
in my throat
from blinding me

To the reality
within the tragedy of
how avoidable
her loss

Literary Cog

Where
in a poet's mind
is there
a place
to call her own
when all that is
seen is everything
without distinctions
or categories
outside
phenomena
in the midst
of the big push-
pull science
of humanity that goes
on without
apparent reason
for its dutiful occupants
most affected
while its restless others
question
everything that is
sacred
or not
if life is to be
sustained as something
of value

and form is to be
given to the life-ful/less
masses
beyond some bold
abomination
marauding away
at the precious vitality
that hangs on
in the balance
precariously teetering
on the verge
of hysteria
amidst its unseen limitations
not at all panacea-like
in nature
still
must the poet seek
to find and identify
that which she sees
and that which she knows
instinctively
to be unyieldingly indifferent
to rhyme or reason
for more than
an instant
in time
on paper

Stained Glass Window

And so
it all relates
back to a face
that does not mirror
mine
love
music
honor
architecture
fine arts
style, history
accomplishment
even
Jesus Christ
none of it
presumably
has anything to do
with me
if I let you
tell it
keeping my hands
tied tightly
behind my back
without protest
Whilst
I remain

a mirror
only
of crime
ignorance
neediness
domesticity
ugliness-
self-hatred

The scapegoat
catching all
the hell
right here on earth
where aliens walk
among me
and don't care
about anything beyond
the two-sided mirror
held tightly
in hand
indifferent
to its reflections

Restorations

There is no pity
in my heart
for you
for there
is no room
amidst
the uncertainty
of a most certain
anger
residing
in close proximity
with resentment
of a beast
far greater
than the bastard child
birthed
by it
nurtured
by it
profiting from
and existing
within its creator's
belly
wantonly reckless
tragically
regurgitated

this particular time
(once again)
in hideous, monstrous
fashion
upon you,
my sister
Therefore
upon me

And I am
visited often
by feelings
of disgust,
blinding pain,
emptiness-
no doubt
from within
your void
We will
both come to know
better
our capacity
for living
despite
the loss

II

Pulse

*Living is serious business and if you're doing it well,
you haven't time for anything else and nothing else is
more satisfying.*

Rise n' Shine

I'm gonna sit
down
and write
myself a poem
in my doom & gloom
proof room

Where the sun comes through
like a charm
does it shine
down

With a new state of mind
I sing
songs inside
my head hungry
for more of
what is
being fed

I'm gonna rise up
after I sit
down
with poem in hand
and light in heart

I'll keep that sun's shine
deep
within me

Still

Still,
You portray Us
In 'advertising' of
All media types
As,
Ecstatic, enthusiastic
'Servants'—
Laborers,
Waiters,
Waitresses,
Bell-'Boys',
Cooks
Housekeepers,
Etcetera...

Nearly all
Of whom,
Are smiling
Too broadly,
Anxiously awaiting
Service to you
Still

Nearly all
Of Us,
You'd like

To lead 'others'
To believe,
Haven't
A propensity
For anything else,
"Useful"

The Remainder
Of Us (of course) being,
Welfare parasites,
Petty thieves,
& Vicious criminals...

The "latest" is,
"We're born that way"

No doubt
Formulated by
The same
'Intellectual Think Tank'
That serves the media
So well

Still

Mind Trippin' Stream of Consciousness In The City On A Friday Evening Rejuvenating On The Couch...

Staring @ a 90 degree angle's impression
of the torchiere's light thrust upward
upon the green walls
like a horizontal sunrise bursting
hearing the slickness of the street under the
rubber
tires of varied sizes
rolling by fast and faster overtop
the rain-moistened asphalt
hearing a horn honking impatiently in urgent
request
of an unknown passenger to be
becoming muted by the noise of my
transitioning
heating unit kick on to counter
prescribed thermostatic limits
becoming infiltrated by night's approach outside
within the walls
listening
tink, tink, tink, tink
Whuuuuuhhhhhhhh
begins the symphony of the blower conductor
further muting all other sounds

becoming the ohm by which I fade
now into the garbled pink wax
of my mood (lava) lamp
more befitting of my mood than looking
like lava
misshapen and floating within the apex
in part
looking as though held fast there
by the less melted, stubborn pink wax
creating an arm projecting from its deep
pink still frozen horizon
holding mass up high
feeling my mind ease then
jolt with the sound of a trucker's horn
sounding warning to potential fools
who would consider crossing it
from a side street
breathing easier now
reluctantly preparing to cleanse the small
mountain of encrusted dishes residing
not so peacefully
inside the sink when the phone rings
in interruption
of needful thoughts of drudgery
beginning the night soon as always
when a Friday comes longed for
as if peace will ride its back
in blissful accompaniment
sometime before Sunday comes
and pressures fade

Laughter

Inhalation
Exhalation

Bellowing...

Up
Out

Articulating earthquakes

Gut to Mouth

Facades dissolve
Amidst its genuineness

Long then after
do we
reminisce

New Race-Ism

If you could
imagine
a chainsaw nearby
in the offing
of a thick wood

you could
imagine
the dull reminder
its presence sounds
now
unseen
heard faintly

imminently
dangerous
to use ear plugs

Deep Cuts

Where is the African-American
Man?

The "black male" is paraded
incessantly

Rarely in form
True to life

Via various mediums
audio and visual

As the 'dark,' black male
with few positive attributes

Purveyor of all things
detrimental

Unless,

Accompanied-
appropriately
by the order-giving

Or,

Beleagured by
expectant
beneficiaries

Of his labors...
Ignored, endless
labors to
"fit in"

Like his sisters, seen
often
in a more positive light-

Coddled
in Mammy
remembrances

Portrayed
by the very media
that douses the fuel

To ignite the flames
to char the flesh
of her

African-American brother
and husband
father and son
uncle and cousin
nephew and grandson...

Domino in its effect
if she is to accept
her 'prescribed' admission

At the expense of her true worth and
the existence of her brother
in hue

Her African-American brother,
who walks the longest mile
of all those who dare persist

In the face of tempestuous winds
which threaten to blind
those willing to confront them

Like they most assuredly
blind the Majority
who do not

As is fitting
accompaniment for paralyzed bodies
housing numbed souls

That
bow to
oppression

And "see"
only

in its wake-
Woefully
inept at navigating
of their own accord

While doing so
adeptly, eagerly
at the expense of

An "other"
expendable
black
male

To quash fires of
their own
self-contempt
and loathing

Short-lived
in relief

Gluttonous
in desire

To exercise
demons
which haunt
minds of the damned

Like those
who see
but do not
see

Instinctively aware
there will come
an End

And with it
a Peace
whose grasp
will ever elude them

Whose taste
they shall never
savor

Concerto

Wondrous eloquence
Spoken not
Through voice
Passages
Nor eyes'
Glimpses

Though carried
Graciously-
Waltzed
Between airs
Separating
Souls, physiologically
Embodied
Yet, emotionally
Rapt

In proximity's
Aura
Intensely magnifying
Virgin Realities

Love Ballad

We greeted
on the floor

Then met
during the dance

Embracing
our minds raced

To quiet
proximity's intensity

Exchanging glances
subtle amid dimly lit surroundings

Paving way
to quickened familiarity

Fostering
proximity's intensity

Words deliberately spoken
without parting lips

Beyond accelerated
needs to breathe

More quietly
down and away

From joined
profiles

Warm with scents
intermingled

Swaying softly,
slowly

Motioning spirited
like hand-held fans

At Sunday summer
service

Intent on discovery
yet needing cool concentration

To visualize
what is already conceived

Anticipating magnitudes
so profound

In scope, dwarfing
proximity's intensity

As harmony takes hold
compelling our rhythmic destiny

Together
long after the dance

Tight

I can squeeze
on a dollar
'til the joker drip
green

If I gotta make it
holler-
Yeah, you know
what I mean

It aint no picnic
countin' chickens
so damn close

When you're faced
with eatin'
tuna
on your luxury toast

But you gotta
get up
on it and keep fuelin'
the fire

'Cause that self-deprivation
you know
gon' take you higher

Than the stuff
you "missin' out on"-
obstacles
to the dream

That's the only vision
my mind has
seen

And until it is
attained
as it will
be

You keep on
makin' dollars
from every
last penny

Eyes fixed
on the future
more clear every second
'cause the alternative
is void
without reason
or direction

III

Compass

You are limited only by your imagination;
If it doesn't go far, neither will you.

The Point

There lies a place
wherein no one can go
but you
if you dare

Existing solely
for the benefit
of bringing back
a self unrecognizeable
prior to making
the journey

It lies within
providing shelter
from reeling uncertainties
plaguing realities
and keenly felt dismay

But
can only be obtained
through earnest desire
guiding into
lighted
passages out of
darkened crevices

Awakening the mind
body and soul
into greater consciousness
of self

Moving
out of surrealistic chains
freeing
the spirit
willing survival
beyond all apparent reason

It exists
for sanity's sake

Arbitrary Disparity

What am I
to think of
this anarchy
I am
expected to live within
where I am expected
to soothe, comfort, diffuse
through God-given gifts
You'd just as soon
I'd squander in efforts
to keep you
soothed, comforted, diffused
by/from/and away
from your haunted past
remaining my modern-day
reality
As I sing you a song
play you a tune
dance a bit-
just enough
to bring egregiously veiled
symptoms of joy
constantly elusive
In truth
as you further beckon
me again
to do your bidding
@ having felt another pang

of disquieted fear-
Revelation
perhaps
My revolution
but not yet
Soon
Still haunting me
in your modern-day
psychosis
to be
the scapegoat
@ all the right times
in all the right places
faces
mirroring me
and mine
find willing audiences
in you and yours
constantly seeking
to silence the blame
though you invented
The Game
boldly bearing
your name
despite your professions
of willful ignorance
paying substantially
with a ransom
not to be
collected or thought about

by Kings and Queens
better
knowing not
to place so precious
their gifts
upon so fleeting an alter
which sinks deeper
with each
accepted denial
shouting loudly
from mouths
contentedly attached
only to deaf ears
and sightful eyes
sewn
meticulously
shut

Reason

I write
I write
because
I must
counter
before I turn
to dust
so very many
ashen stereotypes
forever proliferating
unabated
or negated
despite the multitudes
declaring
themselves intellectual
or rational
not at all
contributing
insight
perhaps for
fear of insight
greater than
what simply is
sought
which cannot
be laid peacefully
to rest
at complacent feet

that move not
the course
of their own direction
and unable to
recognize independent
destinies
without being
told

Thus
I must
labor
pen to paper
as with
machete to cane
clearing
every step
short-sighted but
sure
footed despite
shortness of breath
I write
I write
In vision I write
leaning precariously
into the awakening of
a destiny
that is also
mine

Wreckages

She related the accident
to me how his head hung
tragically out
the rear left passenger
window
behind where he'd been
seated
and further relating
his face–eyes
closed
wearing the only mask
death truly brings
stopping
in mid-sentence
remembering
then further relating
his car
gold with a gold package
—nice car
crushed
by the weight
of the delivery truck
surrealistically imposed
upon its and his
body
simultaneously
listening

hearing
repeating—
...gold with a gold package
—nice car...
the words detouring to
imprisonment of a thought
undying
alive and well before
the scene

who to fault
before untangling the wreckage
in advance of reason
assumptions appearing
glazing over
all else
knowing he was Black
head repeating
...gold with a gold package
—nice car...
now the indicting chorus
before me
The Jury
recognizing
in absolute horror
my own entombment
lacking automatic pilot

for elevation
to justice beyond compassion
or imagery

lacking in judgment
my own skin
without
would scream aloud
with authority
and indignation
on behalf of the very soul
within
head repeating
...gold with a gold package
—nice car...

reeling now
approaching
muted hysteria
with the knowledge
that justice
did not prevail
or compel above all else
as it must
immediately
without question

how it must
be the first thing
past compassion
I seek if at all
I do seek

But never
should its antithesis find me
with the advantage of forethought—
objective and unadorned

But it did!
It snaked in
to an assumed conscious mind

like the grim reaper
did the man
I gave only
the benefit of the doubt
and my compassion
before
the details
surrounding his demise

Losing a portion
of my own self
with him

Molecular Being

I
am this
mass

A living, breathing, thinking
feeling
extraordinary mass

Bound
together in
discord
when harmony eludes
me

Covering
not so
easily
the pain
of being, feeling, thinking, breathing

Extraordinarily incapable
of being
something, everything, anything
else

But capable
of realizing
the enormity of
my deformity

And how alone
it leaves me
to feel
scattered

A View of Africa

Forget...
its relevance
marginal at best
as is its majority
composition
lending nothing physically
tangible
worthwhile
save the diamonds
mined relentlessly
by a marginal majority
too stupid
to pay
closer attention
to its greatest resource
without untold prodigal sons
leading the way
ensuring
captivity
remains
amply unrewarded
bought and paid for
in full
until the money runs
out
or the dark continent
is
no more

Savior

Bird song
sing bird
as you melt
my soul away from this

Place
me in your comfort-
care
a melody you lay
alongside my burdens
heavily down
a much needed reprieve

Bird so beautifully
sing
and melt this cold
soul awake

Reveille

Stuck
voices haunting
calling me
to stop
what I am
thinking
evoking thoughts
of following through
with my life
the way it would be
were it not for
voices haunting
reminding me
of limited choices
offering real security
if I am
to realize any peace
or is it piece?
Stuck
voices haunting
telling me
my way is insane
no one would dare
do as I contemplate
regardless of the need

to create a place
safe and secure
for my self
to abide in
fully
and without
question
or thought of being
Stuck
with voices
haunting me

Ms. Liberty's Stance

See her
fist raised
high
amidst her sky-drop
tower of power

Embodiment of strength
borne to be
A beacon
yet
unimposing in her bronze
enormity

She summons
not one
but all
who dare dream
boldly beyond
meager beginnings
fast-coming forward
moving generations
inside simultaneous
individual struggle

Beckoned onward
still
by her presence
silenced of doubt

inspired in its stead
empowered
by the light
she holds
so visibly
up high

Untouchable
without earnest
desire
still attainable

For all
those who seek
higher grounds
comprising
more
solid foundation

Borne
not of arrogance
or ego
but innate understanding
of a soul's need
to reach
the highest
possible
flight

Flight of The Spirit

I thought about you
Last night

While you were here and
Even more

When you left
There went a piece of

Me
With you

I contemplate it
Over and again

The next morning
And into the night

After night has passed
I'll question again what

I already know
Love beckons me beyond

Where I am
Hopefully not

Hopelessly lost
Never to be found

No Woman-Child Cry

Black Girl
Why is color
on your mind
Don't you know
you can be who
ever you want
to be
whenever
you need to be
Black Girl
Why is color
on your mind
Mammy don't exist
no more
except
in your head
Don't you know
you can be who
ever you want
Black Girl
Why is color
on your mind
all the time
Can't you just forget
the past
and let it be
the past
Black Girl?
Disappear.

Middle Passage

Go young children
and learn

Seek out
those things
which make your spirits
burn

Just go

Learn

Spiral Pillar

Standing still
endeavoring to feel
the abysmal form
within the cavity
of my human frame
straining desperately
to maintain a constant
A self
renewing in fact
but a self
intact
with or without
the manifestations that
pain and self-doubt reveal
to us
all
living outside
our deepest selves
buried
undetectable by the sub-
conscious
levels which ordinarily remind
us
to be us-
but more importantly
for me to be

me
in tact
in spite
of the deference
in spite
of the indifference-
a writer
a poet
a person
a woman
a Black, strong, writer, poet, person
woman
capable
but willfully limiting
a self
that must express
all
a self
that is
to be explored
and revealed
despite
the onslaught
the implication
the negativity
the audacity
that speaking about such

that speaking about me
for me
without regard
for reprisal
obstacles created to shore up
progress
with this angst
that must be removed
if I am
if I am
if I am
I must endeavor
still
to delve deeper
still
I must look
where the hurt is sure
to face me
to chide me
to infuriate me
in the face of all
things
that plague me
I must endeavor
deeper
into the abyss

the darkness
inside myself
that lurks shamefully
about the sub
of my conscious
where I unwittingly
discard it
until such time as I gather
the necessary tools
to mine
the diamond in the rough
I've always known
lay in wait
The gem of the ages
that is cut solely
for me
from me
and my existence
Black
like the onyx
shining
without polish
Set in stone
if the abysmal trip
is avoided-
thus I endeavor
finding out

truths, told and silent
no less evident
Facing them
in the midst of my own
uncertainty
knowing that it is
because of that uncertainty
that I must
endeavor
Looking
into the glass
mirror
television
windows that hold no images
of me
quite recognizable
by me
Wondering when
if I do not
endeavor
to labor
as with this poem
will there ever be
a song for me
that mammy did not first sing
to Suzy and John

and when
if ever
if I do not endeavor
will there ever be
a young Black girl
who is comfortable
being a young
Black
Girl
without having first to sing
the song of a piper
who serves her misery
at not being able to conform
to an impossible
image
created outside herself
yet adopted
like some tragic orphan
dropped from the acid rain
which can only be handled
with kid-gloves
and whom no one else cares for
regardless of the weather
And when
if ever does a child
like that have the opportunity
to be reminded of anything

that may mirror in the glass
or the television screen
Some one
instead of
some thing
inhuman or superhuman
exotic-dark
something to be conquered
like a forbidden land
by her blanched counter part
regarding her highly
in concubinal terms
while her
brother in hue
sees only her image
as something nearly but not quite
(unless extremely light
or having good hair)
what he would
rather she be
despite the fact
that it is in fact
she
who has brought him here
And when
if ever

if I do not endeavor
will the question
of my existence
here
on earth
around the world
in every capacity
be seen and understood
as more than
a mere passing presence
born for the taking
only of my wisdom
and exterior component
without regard
for the soul
that attaches undividedly
to the body
for all mine
and my ancestor's
born days
reborn in me
and me through them
passing on
in body
but never in spirit
unburdened with each breath
I take

in effort
to make
this life
my life
more meaningful
than that
which you would assign me
if I did not
so endeavor
as now

Waste Not

With a mind
to do so
I can
do anything
with a mind to
do
so I can
do anything
with a mind
to
do so
I
can do
anything
with my mind
I can
do anything
at all
I put my mind
to

IV

Haiku

(A Japanese minimalist form of poetry, maintaining a 5/7/5 syllable stanza discipline.)

Believing is stronger than hope.

Skin

Permanently yours
Despite its shade or texture
Reveals nothing more

Life

A process to live
Often existed within
Defying purpose

Shame

Hidden from full view
Unwittingly acting out
Painful memories

Hope

Inward compulsions
Moving toward renewal
Spiritually

Homeless

Hushed desperation
Mortality realized
Vulnerable one

Hands

Lovingly caress
Bridging indifferences
Soothingly away

Addiction

Unequaled cravings
Obliviate obstacles
Outside objective

Nigger

Unfairly leveled
Ignorance personified
By group assumption

Change

Occurs regardless
Received best when understood
Facilitates growth

On Life's Process...

Seek to close open circles, dot your i's, cross your t's, put back where you found, maintain commitments and by all means—broaden your horizons.

—M. Rose Barkley

If you know someone who would benefit from *Wayfaring Stranger*, you can order more copies of this book by filling out the following information:

Send _____ copies of *Wayfaring Stranger*.

(Please Print)

Name:_____

Address _____

City _____State_____ Zip _____

Cost: Single copy $11.95 (US) $ _____

Virginia residents add 4.5% sales tax   _____

Shipping & handling:

    $3.50 for up to 2 books   _____

Plus $1.25 for each additional book   _____

Total Enclosed $ _____

Please send check or money order to:

sound publishing co.

Sound Publishing Co.

P.O. Box 26782

Richmond, VA 23261

Phone: 804-783-9673

Fax: 804-648-8855

To have M. Rose Barkley speak to your organization, please call, write or fax.